Grand Teton National Park is a land of contrasts. Vast landscapes and intimate forests, narrow canyons and open sky, sagebrush-covered valley and towering mountain range are all part of this spectacular place. Such diversity provides habitat for many wildlife species including moose, elk, bison, bears, coyotes, eagles, waterfowl, and songbirds. It is a place where songs of the wild can still be heard.

Light adds to the changing moods of the Tetons.
Warm rich sunlight seems to bring the peaks
even closer to the valley, while gray shadows create
a distant elusive mood.

Front cover: The Tetons in autumn, photo by Larry Ulrich. Inside front cover: Arrowleaf balsamroot, Jackson Lake, and the Tetons, photo by Russ Finley. Page 1: Bull moose feeding in Snake River, photo by Jeff Vanuga. Pages 2/3: North face of the Grand Teton, photo by Ed Cooper. Pages 4/5: Jackson Lake and the Teton Range, photo by Salvatore Vasapolli.

Grand Teton National Park, *located in northwestern Wyoming, was established in 1929 to protect the Teton Range and the lakes below.*

Edited by Cheri C. Madison.
Book design by K. C. DenDooven.

Second Printing, 1998

in pictures GRAND TETON: The Continuing Story
© 1995 KC PUBLICATIONS, INC.

*"The Story Behind the Scenery"; "in pictures... The Continuing Story";
the parallelogram forms and colors within are registered
in the U.S. Patent and Trademark Office.*

LC 95-75097. ISBN 0-88714-084-X.

in pictures
Grand Teton
The Continuing Story®

by Jackie Gilmore

Since 1978, Jackie Gilmore has worked as a freelance writer, photographer, and naturalist in Jackson Hole, Wyoming. Her work has been published in many national and regional publications. She has a master's degree in environmental education and is currently on the faculty of Teton Science School in Grand Teton National Park.

*National park areas
are special landscapes set aside
by acts of Congress to protect
and preserve features of national
significance that are generally
categorized as scenic, scientific,
historical, and recreational.*

*As Americans, we are joint
caretakers of these unique places,
and we gladly share them with
visitors from around the world.*

The Tetons rise over a mile above
the valley floor, and their jagged
peaks stand against the sky with
authority. Shining lakes and
meandering creeks, towering trees
and colorful wildflowers, eagles
and elk fill the valley below with
the energy of life. In 1929, the Teton
Range and the lower lakes were
given national park status; in 1950,
valley and river lands were added
to the park. Quiet contemplation
and grand dreams fit into the
landscape as this stunning scenery
invites you to sit quietly along the
river's edge or to stand above the
world on a mountain peak.

JOHN P. GEORGE

*The restless gray skies of an autumn
storm and golden aspen leaves make
dramatic partners.*

7

▲ **Throughout winter, the** *snow pack is one to four feet deep in the valley and up to eight and one-half feet in the mountains.*

◀ **In a serene backwater** *area of the Snake River, a beaver pond creates a mirror of the Tetons.*

The Tetons

Change is the constant in the Tetons, from the variety of topography to the seasonal climate. In the highest reaches of the park, glacial lakes are nestled below rock amphitheaters and the high trails wander through lovely alpine meadows where stunted plants grow quickly in the brief summer warmth. At the foot of the Tetons, the valley known as Jackson Hole stretches for miles. The climate in the Tetons offers variety, too, from frigid winter weather to temperate summer days. In the early 1800s, fur trappers frequented the valley in search of beavers. Valleys surrounded by mountains were called "holes" by trappers, and they named this area Jackson's Hole after trapper David E. Jackson. The first homesteaders arrived in 1884, and cattle ranching was their primary livelihood. Dude ranching and hunting attracted tourists in the 1920s, and over the years the number of visitors has steadily increased. Now, more than 3 million people visit the park each year.

The Grand Teton is the highest peak in the Teton Range at an elevation of 13,770 feet, and Mt. Owen is 12,928 feet high. Views of these two peaks from both the east and west sides illustrate the rugged rock environment found at this elevation. As you move north or south along the east side of the range, the peaks seem to change size depending on your location.

◁ **R**ugged peaks offer access to distant views of Jackson Hole and the surrounding mountains.

PAUL DIX

Jackson Lake is almost 17 miles long, with a maximum depth of approximately 437 feet. An aerial view of Moran Bay in Jackson Lake dramatically illustrates the difference in elevation between the mountains and the valley.

Wildlife at Grand Teton in All Seasons

Observing wildlife in Grand Teton can be one of the most rewarding and exciting activities for the alert and patient observer. Wildlife most frequently seen in the sagebrush-grassland valley includes pronghorn, elk, bison, coyotes, Uinta ground squirrels, and badgers. Mule deer, porcupines, red squirrels, snowshoe hares, and black bears spend summers in the forests. Moose, beavers, river otters, and muskrats can often be observed in wetlands along the lakes, rivers, and creeks. Most of the mammal species stay in the valley throughout winter, and each species has its own adaptations to help survive the difficult conditions. Moose, deer, elk, bison, and coyotes move to areas where snow depth is relatively low so they can find food. Black bears, ground squirrels, and marmots hibernate in dens or underground burrows. Porcupines, red squirrels, and martens are active throughout winter, and pikas and beavers rely on stored food to eliminate the need to be out and about above the snow. Nearly 200 species of birds live part or all of the year in Jackson Hole including bald eagles, trumpeter swans, sandhill cranes, great blue herons, Canada geese, several species of waterfowl, hummingbirds, and songbirds. Most birds migrate out of the valley for winter, but some species remain including the eagle, swan, raven, chickadee, and gray jay.

D. ROBERT FRANZ

◁ **M**oose spend winter in wetlands that provide willows for food, and they browse on bitterbrush that grows among sagebrush. Their long legs help them move about in deep snow, and a thick undercoat of hair provides insulation from the cold. Bull moose shed their antlers in December and January.

△ **C**anada geese are common on lakes and in grasslands where they graze. They nest as soon as the ground is free of snow, and downy yellow goslings hatch in May. Large numbers of Canada geese spend fall on Jackson Lake.

Least chipmunks are equally at home in trees or on the ground where they eat seeds, fruits, and other plant material. ▽

SCOTT PRICE

DIANA STRATTON

△ **B**eavers use their sturdy chisel-shaped front teeth to cut willow branches and fall aspen and cottonwood trees. They eat the bark, then use the stripped branches and trunks in the construction of dams and lodges. When beavers dam a stream, wetlands are enhanced providing habitat for other wildlife such as moose, trumpeter swans, ducks, and geese.

13

▲ **Pronghorns (often called antelope) spend summer in sagebrush-grasslands. Fawns (usually** twins) *are born in late May and early June, and in about six weeks the tiny fawns can run along with the herd. Pronghorns arrive in the valley in May and migrate back to southern Wyoming in fall.*

Creatures Big...

Rocky Mountain ▷
elk are found throughout the park in summer. Cows and calves usually stay in shady forests during the day, moving into open meadows in the evening to graze. Bull elk summer alone or in small groups. Most park elk migrate to the National Elk Refuge, north of the town of Jackson, for winter.

JEFF VANUGA

△ **In the fall, bull moose** seek out individual cows to mate. They may stay with a single cow for several days and defend her from other bulls. Equally matched bulls will spar with antlers to determine who wins the right to a cow. Calves are born in May or June.

Black bears are ▷ opportunistic feeders and eat grasses, berries, carrion, and a variety of other foods. Although black bears can be black, brown, or tawny in color, those in the western United States are most commonly brown.

MICHAEL H. FRANCIS

△ **River otters live along lakes, rivers, and streams.** Excellent underwater swimmers, they can stay submerged for two to three minutes. They spend much of their time playing with each other in the water and cavorting along the bank.

JEFF VANUGA

△ **The coyote's howl is a reminder of** the wildness still present on our earth. In mid-summer, pups begin to practice their howling techniques, yipping jubilantly along with the adults.

JEFF VANUGA

△ **Pikas live on rocky slopes where they use the** natural tunnels for shelter. They store plants underneath boulders for a winter food supply and remain active under the deep snow pack.

JEFF VANUGA

△ **Male elk, deer, and moose grow a new set** of antlers each year and shed them in winter. Shed antlers provide calcium for small mammals such as the chipmunk, mice, and porcupines.

KENT & DONNA DANNEN

KENT & DONNA DANNEN

JEFF FOOTT

△ **A** *badger's long claws and powerful legs*
help it dig into burrows at an amazing speed in
pursuit of ground squirrels.

M*uskrats are common along waterways that provide*
aquatic plants for food. In the park, they live mostly in
bank dens and only occasionally build the familiar
muskrat house seen in other parts of the country. ▽

DIANA STRATTON

And Birds, Too

△ **The killdeer uses this "broken wing" behavior** to lead predators away from its nest which is built on rocky ground and made of a few small pebbles.

△ **Great horned owls are active mostly at night.** During the day, they roost in conifer trees next to the trunk. The first primary feather on each wing is serrated to allow silent flight as they hunt.

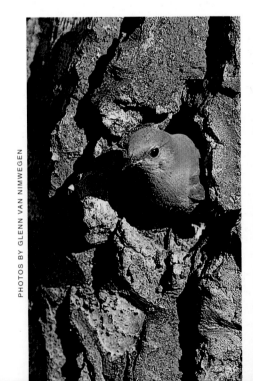

◁ **Mountain bluebirds nest in** tree cavities, often using those excavated by woodpeckers. The cup-shaped nest is made of pine needles, twigs, grass, and plant stems. Bluebirds usually raise two broods each year, with four to eight nestlings each time. When the eggs hatch, both male (left) and female (right) are busy during daylight hours taking insects to their hungry young.

KENT & DONNA DANNEN

MICHAEL H. FRANCIS

△ **C**lark's nutcrackers use their sturdy bills to crack open pine and other conifer cones in order to retrieve the seeds at the base of the scales.

△ **S**age grouse congregate in small groups for courtship rituals. The male inflates a sac in his neck and fans his erect tail to attract females.

SCOTT PRICE

Trumpeter swans are the largest waterfowl in North America with a weight of 20 to 30 pounds and a wingspan of 8 feet. They feed in shallow water by tipping over to reach for plants on the muddy bottom. The reddish neck color is stain ▽ from minerals in the mud.

GLENN VAN NIMWEGEN

△ **M**ale yellow-headed blackbirds have bright yellow heads, while the female is brown with a yellowish throat. They nest in marshes and attach their nests to vegetation such as cattails that grow above the water.

PATRICK CONE

▲ **Lodgepole pine forests cover a substantial** portion of the lower mountain slopes and parts of the valley floor. The seedlings grow quickly and thrive in the open sun. Lodgepoles are small, slender trees and rarely grow taller than 75 feet in this area. Native American Indians used the trunks of small trees to make frames for their lodges or "tepees."

JOHN P. GEORGE

▲ **The small cones of spruce trees have thin,** flexible, paper-like scales in contrast to the woody scales of pine cones. Blue spruce usually grow below the 6,800-foot elevation and are common along the Snake River bottom, while Engelmann spruce grow above elevations of 6,800 feet in mountain canyons. Chipmunks, squirrels, and birds eat spruce seeds.

CARL URSANEN

△ **T**he rough reddish-brown
bark of this limber pine
deepens in color with the
warm sunset light.

DIANA STRATTON

Some lodgepole pine ▷
cones are dependent on
the hot temperatures of
fires to spread their seeds.
These serotinous cones
are tightly closed and
protected with a waxy
covering. The cones
remain closed until
temperatures of at least
113°F are present, then
pop open to release the
seeds. This adaptation
provides instant reseeding
after a fire.

JACKIE GILMORE

The Diversity of Life

LORRI FRANZ

△ **T**he golden-mantled ground squirrel lives in rocky areas. Its diet includes fungi, plants, seeds, insects, eggs, and carrion.

△ **T**he variety of habitats in the park provide intimate settings for wildlife observations. The evening sun backlights the beautiful soft velvet-covered antlers of this mule deer buck. He has come to a tiny pond to drink and will slip back into the forest in the evening shadows.

Shallow braided channels, ▷ fast-moving flat water, peaceful backwaters, and roaring whitewater characterize the spectacular Snake River. With headwaters in southern Yellowstone National Park, the river winds through Grand Teton from the north, flows through Jackson Hole, through Idaho, and into Washington where it joins the Columbia River.

22

GLENN VAN NIMWEGEN

JOHN P. GEORGE

△ **B**ald eagles nest along rivers and lakes. *The nests, which are used year after year, can be 12 feet deep and 7 to 8 feet across.*

△ **T**he snow palette reveals the comings and *goings of wildlife that winter in the valley.*

Overleaf: Jackson Lake was enlarged ▷ *in the early 1900s when its outlet was dammed for irrigation in Idaho. Photo by Dick Dietrich.*

Bison were in the valley hundreds of years ago, but were not present when white settlers arrived. In 1968, *9 bison escaped from the Jackson Hole Wildlife Park, located near the Jackson Lake Dam, where they were kept on display. They remained free to sire the present herd of about 130 individuals. Bison spend summer along the* ▽ *river bottoms and in sagebrush flats and grasslands. They migrate to the National Elk Refuge for winter.*

In the Depth of Winter

Ice crystals reflect sunlight to
*create this unique effect. Parhelions are on
the right and left of the center cross, which
is formed at the juncture of a horizontal
sunstreak and a vertical sun pillar.*

◁ **In winter, animals**
*limit their movement to
reduce the expenditure
of calories. Disturbance
to wintering wildlife
which forces them to
expend extra energy can
be a serious threat to
their survival.*

Wind is an ▷

*ever-present element
winter, swirling the snow
through the air, pushing
into huge drifts, an
packing the flakes int
artistic designs*

DIANA STRATTON

26

Moisture-laden air ▷ *combined with frigid night temperatures produces a heavy coating of frost on every element in the landscape. These conditions exist only a few weeks each winter. A close look at this frost reveals intricate edges and delicate formations beyond the imagination.*

DIANA STRATTON

JEFF FOOTT

The Grand Teton and most of
the surrounding smaller peaks are
composed of granite which, from a
distance, appears whiter than gneiss.
Gneisses make up the main rock
masses in the Teton Range. The
mineral content of gneiss varies which
results in light gray, white, dark gray,
dark green, and black rocks.

◁ **T**he rock wall at the head of a
glacier is called a cirque. These steep
walls are cut by the glacier at its thickest
point and are further carved by frost
action. A glacial lake is created when the
glacier cuts a shallow basin at the bottom
of the cirque, then melts.

The Forces

For millions of years, geologic forces have been at work creating the Teton Range and Jackson Hole as we know them today. Over the last 2.5 billion years, ancient oceans, volcanic activity, and the intrusion of shallow inland seas contributed to changes in the character of this region. The formation of the Teton Range began about 9 million years ago as earthquakes occurred along the Teton fault. As a result of many large earthquakes, the land block on the west side swung upwards to form the mountains, while the east block dropped to create the valley. The total vertical movement along the fault has been about 30,000 feet, and the downward movement of the valley block has been about four times greater than the upward movement of the mountain block. Over time, the valley has been filled in with volcanic ash from Yellowstone, glacial deposits, and erosion debris, so that today there is only a 6,000- to 7,000-foot difference in elevation between the valley floor and the Teton summits. Three periods of glaciation, erosion, frost wedging, and avalanches have further contributed to the shaping of the land. The mountains and valley continue their vertical movement along the fault; and water, wind, ice, and snow continue to add their touches to the landscape of the Tetons and Jackson Hole.

ED COOPER

***W*hen spring comes to Jackson Hole,** ▷
the snow melts quickly and rushing waters carve the canyons deeper. Cascade Creek flows through Cascade Canyon, plunges 200 feet down Hidden Falls, and finally joins Jenny Lake on the valley floor.

Building Lakes

A *glacier is a massive moving ice sheet formed when more*
snow falls than melts over time. As a glacier moves slowly downslope scouring
and cutting the mountain, it picks up rocks and debris. When it
reaches a valley, it often scoops out a basin before it begins to melt.
The piles of debris left behind after a glacier melts are called moraines. Lateral
moraines are those formed along the sides of the glacier, while the terminal moraine is the
pile left at the front of the glacier when it stops. The glacier acts like a conveyer belt,
moving forward and dropping the rocks as it reaches the end point, thus creating a
dam-like structure. During the third period of glaciation in the Tetons, about 20,000 years
ago, glaciers flowed down the east side of the Teton Range and into the valley.
At higher elevations there are many small lakes created by glaciers, such as Lake Solitude.
On or near the valley floor, glaciers created the larger lakes including Phelps, Taggart,
Bradley, Jenny, String, and Leigh. The terminal moraines at the ends of these lower lakes
support forests because they contain moisture-retaining silt
and clay and more nutrients for plant growth.

Extreme changes in temperature cause contraction and expansion in rocks which eventually weakens them. The rocks crack, moisture trapped in the cracks freezes, and the ice pries the rock apart. This frost wedging can break off boulder-sized pieces of rock which tumble downslope hundreds or thousands of feet.

DIANA STRATTON

From the top of Snow King Mountain, the view to the north includes the town of Jackson, the Gros Ventre Buttes, Blacktail Butte, and Grand Teton National Park. The buttes, tilted and faulted masses of rock, were shaped by glaciers as they moved slowly down the valley.

Living with Geologic Change

Large individual ▷ boulders are often seen lying on the valley floor far from the mountain slopes. Some have rolled from high peaks after being dislodged by earthquakes. Others, known as "erratics," have been deposited by glaciers. They may be partially covered by soil that has accumulated over thousands of years.

MARK E. GIBSON

*F*ifty million cubic yards of debris broke loose from Sheep Mountain on June 23, 1925, and slid at 50 miles per hour. Three minutes later, there was a one-mile-long, half-mile-wide scar on the mountainside instead of a forested slope. The debris dammed the Gros Ventre River, impounding water to create Lower Slide Lake. Factors that probably contributed to this massive landslide were saturated ▽ soil from fast-melting snow and heavy rains, and earthquake tremors.

People at Grand Teton

There are countless ways to enjoy Grand Teton National Park, and the diversity of land and life in the park gives visitors the opportunity to experience the natural world with all their senses. Floating down the Snake River, wildlife watching, or wandering aimlessly through wildflower meadows can provide days upon days of respite from the busier world. Steep vertical mountains challenge the best of climbers and miles of backcountry trails offer endless days of solitude. The short steep trail to Hidden Falls and Inspiration Point gives visitors with limited time an opportunity to experience a lush mountain canyon and sparkling waterfall. Longer walks take the hiker to quiet alpine lakes or along the forested paths of the larger lakes on the valley floor. A picnic at String Lake, a lazy summer day on the shores of Jackson Lake, or flyfishing the clear clean waters are wonderful ways to let your mind mingle with the mountains.

PHILIP BOBROW

△ **D**ramatic lighting and colorful subject matter provide stunning images for any photographer.

A scenic float trip on the Snake River is an ideal way to get in touch with the rhythms of the river. ▽ The Tetons provide dramatic scenery, and wildlife is often observed from the raft.

△ **T**his climber used an ice axe for safety to cross Teepe Glacier. There are about a dozen small reestablished glaciers in the Teton Range, many of which can be seen from the valley floor.

◁ **W**ith miles of trails, the Tetons invite backcountry hiking. A use permit is required for all overnight trips. Some campsites are available on a reservation basis, while others are "first-come, first-served."

◁ Sheer granite faces challenge △ ▷

he accomplished mountain climber, and
ovices can find a wide choice of less technical
limbs. On the mountain summits, climbers are
ewarded with a sweeping view of Jackson
ole, surrounding mountain ranges, and the
outhern end of Yellowstone National Park.
oor weather can be a factor in any month,
nd rockfalls and avalanches are common.
Mid-July through late September usually offers
he best climbing conditions. Climbing instruc-
on at all levels and climbing guides are avail-
ble in the park.

***K**ayaking in the* ▷ *park can be an all-day adventure or a quiet way to spend a morning. Non-motorized boats are allowed on the Snake River and on some lakes. Boating information can be obtained at park headquarters.*

***F**rom June through August, columbines grace* ▽ *canyon trails, streamsides, and moist meadows.*

ED COOPER

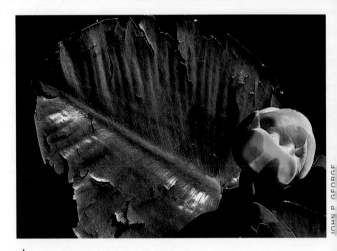

JOHN P. GEORGE

△ ***Y**ellow pondlily flowers have a long stem* *that is attached to a rootstalk buried in the muddy bottom.*

DIANA STRATTON

◁ ***F**rom July through September, the purple flowers of fringed gentians brighten willow patches near Jackson Lake Lodge.*

▲ **High altitude and clean air create many days of clear blue skies in the Tetons, but the elevation and** the mountains contribute to unpredictable weather conditions. Late afternoon thunderstorms brew over the summits in summer, and snowstorms in the high mountains can happen in any month.

JOHN P. GEORGE

JACKIE GILMORE

▲ **Yarrow flowers provide a plentiful food** source for spring azure butterflies.

◁ **The striped coralroot orchid is a splendid** discovery. It has no chlorophyll, and so it uses underground stems to absorb nutrients from decaying organic matter.

JOHN P. GEORGE

DIANA STRATTON

△ **A**spen leaves, attached to the flat stem a an angle, tremble in the slightest breeze.

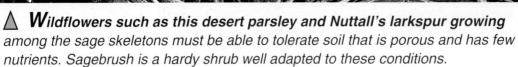

△ **W**ildflowers such as this desert parsley and Nuttall's larkspur growing among the sage skeletons must be able to tolerate soil that is porous and has few nutrients. Sagebrush is a hardy shrub well adapted to these conditions.

Mushrooms ▷ assist with the decay of dead forest plants as they help break down the rotting wood.

40

▲ **The native elk thistle provides food for** wildlife. Elk avidly seek out these thistles for fall forage, and black and grizzly bears eat them, too. Native American Indians used the stems and roots for food, and an early explorer in Yellowstone supposedly survived on them for a month while he was lost.

▲ **The Oregon grape, which prefers well-drained** soil, grows on forested moraines around the valley lakes. This low-growing shrub has clusters of yellow blossoms in spring which yield dark blue berries in August. Although the berries are bitter, they are used by some to make jelly and jam.

◁ **This cabin was built by** Pierce and Margaret Cunningham who homesteaded 160 acres in 1890. The cabin has two log rooms joined by a single roof and an open veranda in the middle to provide ventilation. The logs were notched to fit at the corners, and the cracks were chinked with mud.

▲ **Colter Bay Marina is one**
of three public marinas on
Jackson Lake. Because the wind
can quickly whip up whitecaps
on the lake and the water is very
cold, boaters should exercise
caution while on these or any
park waters. A variety of boats
can be rented at the marinas
including canoes, motorboats,
and pontoon boats.

Lake trout is the ▷
catch of the day on
many Jackson Lake
fishing trips. National
park and state
regulations help protect
the water quality and
fish populations that
are essential to the
survival of many other
species such as bald
eagles, river otters, and
great blue herons.

△ **Cross-country skiing is a popular winter activity in the park. There are many mountain trails to** ski, and the more popular routes such as the Taggart Lake trail are tracked by skiers. For those who enjoy wide-open terrain, most of the valley is accessible. In winter, the inside park road is closed to autos from the Taggart trail area north to Signal Mountain Lodge, and skiing and snowmobiling are allowed. To protect wintering wildlife, river bottoms are closed to all winter use.

The Chapel of the Transfiguration was established in 1925 to serve people who lived north of the town of Jackson. Sunday services are held throughout summer, and the building is open daily. The simple log design and view of the Tetons invite visitors to spend time in quiet contemplation. ▽

▲ *The only native fish in the park is a unique race of* cutthroat, the Snake River cutthroat. Introduced fish include the Rocky Mountain whitefish and lake, rainbow, brown, and brook trout.

SUGGESTED READING

CRAIGHEAD, JR., FRANK C. *For Everything There is a Season: The Sequence of Natural Events in the Grand Teton and Yellowstone Area.* Helena, Montana: Falcon Press, 1994.

CRANDALL, HUGH. *Grand Teton: The Story Behind the Scenery.* Las Vegas, Nevada: K.C. Publications, 1978.

HARRY, BRYAN. *Teton Trails.* Moose, Wyoming: Grand Teton Natural History Association, 1987 (revised edition).

HAYDEN, ELIZABETH WIED. *From Trapper to Tourist.* Moose, Wyoming: Grand Teton Natural History Association, 1981 (revised edition).

OLSON, LINDA L., AND TIM BYWATER. *A Guide to Exploring Grand Teton National Park.* Salt Lake City, Utah: RNM Press, 1991.

Grand Teton Natural History Association

National Park Cooperating Associations were established early in Park Service history as public demand increased for written materials on national parks. Grand Teton Natural History Association (GTNHA), founded in 1937, provides an ever-expanding number of interpretive and educational publications to visitors of Grand Teton National Park. With increased visitation, requests for association funding to augment federal budgets also increase. Profits from bookstores provide funding to Grand Teton National Park for renovation of visitor centers; printing expenses for the park newspaper, the "Teewinot," and thousands of free maps and informational leaflets; exhibits in visitor centers and on trails; supplies for campfire programs; stipends for ranger-naturalist internships; and varied research projects.

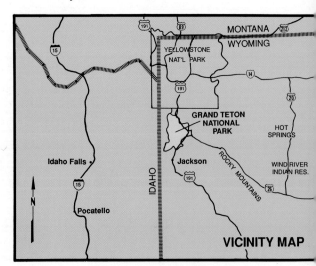

VICINITY MAP

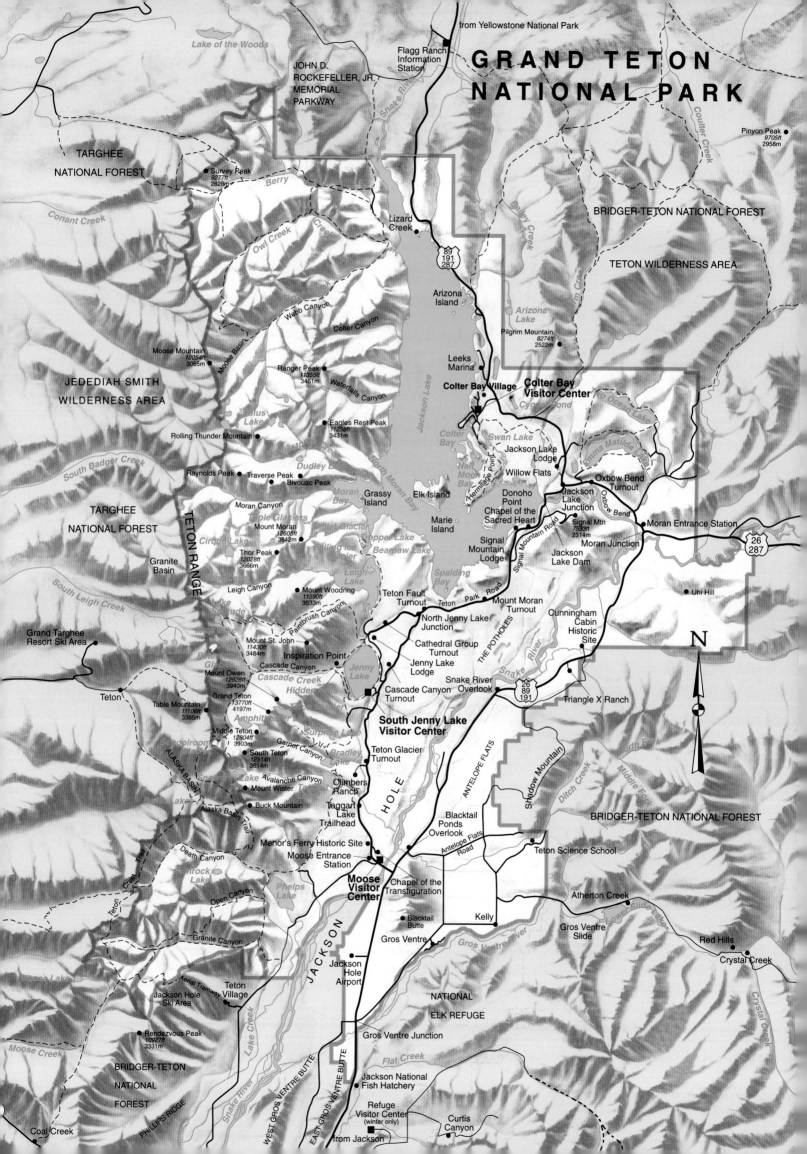

LARRY ULRICH

The magnificent mountain scenery is a delight to the eyes whether it glistens white with snow or glows in warm autumn colors. Fragrant wildflowers, soft summer winds, the coyote's howl, and the bugle of elk in autumn become part of the Teton experience. Whether floating the river as it moves powerfully along its course or standing in a high alpine meadow at dawn, one can become aware of the gifts of our earth. Our national parks give us places where we can encounter nature in our own way and on our own time. They are places where we can allow weather, wildlife, intimate scenes, and dramatic landscapes to fill our senses and our thoughts, places where we can reconnect with the earth and the wildness within ourselves. David Brower encouraged us to preserve our wild places when he said, "Wilderness will belong to all if man also resolves to keep it flowing on, a living gift for all tomorrows."

The autumn colors of cottonwood trees add drama to the valley landscape.

ERWIN & PEGGY BAUER

▲ **As summer ends and autumn colors glow across the valley, the mood shifts as nature** *prepares for winter. Leaves fall, ponds and lakes grow ice skins, and frost greets the early morning sun.*

Inside back cover: *The Tetons at dawn from Snake River Overloc Photo by Glenn Van Nimwege*

Back cover: *Bull moose in Grand Teton National Pa Photo by Russ Finle*

Books in this *"in pictures ... The Continuing Story"* **series are:** Arches & Canyonlands, Bryce Canyon, Crater Lake, Death Valley, Everglades, Glacier, Glen Canyon-Lake Powell, Grand Canyon, Grand Teton, Hawai`i Volcanoes, Mount Rainier, Mount St. Helens, Olympic, Petrified Forest, Rocky Mountain, Sequoia & Kings Canyon, Yellowstone, Yosemite, Zion.

Translation Packages are also available. Each title can be ordered with a booklet in German, French, or Japanese bound into the center of the English book. Selected titles in both this series and our other books are available in up to 8 languages.

The original National Park series, "The Story Behind the Scenery," covers over 75 parks and related areas. Other series include one on **Indian culture,** and the **"Voyage of Discovery"** series on the expansion of the western United States. To receive our catalog with over 110 titles:

Call (800-626-9673), fax (702-433-3420), or write to the address below.

Published by KC Publications, 3245 E. Patrick Ln., Suite A, Las Vegas, NV 89120.

Created, Designed, and Published in the U.S Printed by Doosan Dong-A Co., Ltd., Seoul, Ko Paper produced exclusively by Hankuk Paper Mfg. Co., L